BITTER GREEN

Cover painting: "Kew from Strand-on-the-Green,"
Martin Corless-Smith, oil on canvas. 6 x 8 inches, 2008.
Collection of the Artist.

Book design by Rebecca Wolff

Published in the United States by Fence Books
Science Library, 320
University at Albany
1400 Washington Avenue, Albany, NY 12222

www.fenceportal.org

This book was printed by Versa Press and distributed by
Small Press Distribution and Consortium Book Sales and
Distribution.

Library of Congress Cataloguing in Publication Data
Corless-Smith, Martin [1965–]
Bitter Green/Martin Corless-Smith

Library of Congress Control Number: 2015952297

ISBN 13: 978-1-934200-98-8

First Edition
10 9 8 7 6 5 4 3 2

Fence Books are published in partnership with the
University at Albany and the New York State Writers
Institute, and with invaluable support from the New
York State Council on the Arts and the National
Endowment for the Arts.

Versions of some of these poems appeared in the journals
Bestoned, Cloud Rodeo, No Infinite, Pallaksch, and
Sundial. "A note on Absence" appeared in the "Poem-a-
day" series curated by the Academy of American Poets.

<u>Thank you.</u>

And so, again, withdrew
Himself upon some scene
An attic faith—A dream
Of having passed this way
Angel below—billowing day
I have no strength, no sense
No self—and so

—W. W.

BITTER GREEN

Martin Corless-Smith

FENCE BOOKS

Albany, New York

…pulvis et umbra sumus.
—Horace, Ode IV.7

ouvrir ouvrir the nightingale
how has it come to this?
love is a severed foot
cattled in the guts
a trifle flipped
love is a tree of apricots
all rotted
I can see
it breathe I think
how has it come to this?
the fruit my bliss disdained
a trifle shattered in the breeze

The thistle looking over fields
do not forget the instant of its pink foulard
late in the afternoon when
a single look from her
lifted the torment for a while

When vice may move
before all reckoning my sense
(these are the phantoms
with obscene nick-names)
that outside life is made
profane—and I have written
my own curse for other mouths and mine.

Presents

a mild and moony interlude

Happy when alone and not myself

My knowledge of the world is from the world

The reality of the present consists in the absence of a qualifying prefix

The pastness of an event is not the same thing as the event itself

Lying dead in the kitchen—out of place

Is your hope in retreat—falling to shadows

The last is the song of an exile

When I first lost hold of the thought for a while I still imagined that I might regain it at any instant

What happens to the light inside you

When you love, perhaps an equilibrium of exchange

When you are not around I forget what I might mean to you

You might notice a detail like the trouser leg pulled away from a shin

Perhaps the book will be understood

That which is other of course remains always other

Unknown. Bring your hands together in prayer or
applause

Snowing at night—deep green

Ice cold feet of a statue

Human-skinned flowers, carnations, white poppies.

The boat, the book, the milky eyeless ocean

A decaying whale blossoms into rainbows

Fish in great society ignorant of land

The mouth on both sides of the body sack

If you were to focus on Nativity, Mortality, Change

I shall never have done seeing myself in the past

Orpheus in the forest. Anon among the dolphins

Happily together in an untidy little sitting room
called Confusion Hall

I have no idea what I have written

The severed foot in my stomach is love

We estimate the distances between soldiers

Wednesday, the upper world was utterly bereft

They simply slowly pushed her towards the door

The most important nouns filled with images of the deceased

Strange piping voices one could not quite make out

We see with one eye and stand upon one leg

Whispering push the glass aside

Three bodies hung with clothes

All this time a boat drifting somewhere on the green

<u>A note on Absence</u>

The story over having wished it otherwise

The water surface/friendship

The drunk euphoric

Good Friday music

Not in this lifetime

A fig tree grows

No miserable deed will do

Space and time, dimensions that just bring
more of this

For anyone who has a nose

Show gratitude

A king sat in a box

8 p.m. Friday

rain defeating snow

a space too narrow to pass through

A gannet thru the oil cannot
and a linnet sans a song
the winter is of every count
the water without ground
a fast returning past that
halts the future in her backwards glance
where through a dark gulf I have found
you in your absence always one last breath
through fire without air and earth
forever bitten through my hand.

Nothing has transcended Death

This is the year (it isn't or it's not)
—assertion of material
—a dedication hopeful of eternity
or immortality—Emptiness enharbours all.

—

Descending on a hill in York
a Worcester Market or
The Library in Oxfordshire
Nothing has transmuted emptiness
Nothing has transcended death
A fee paid to a clergyman
all words lacking identity
affirming only their obscurity
Nothing has obliterated God
Nothing has replaced the earth
Nothing now deserves the empty dead
Nothing can unearth our buried hopes
Nothing transfigures eternal woe
The Nothing we have found
as fundamental to our consciousness and soul
the idle body settles after war
slowly the giant corpse supported by its bulk
gives way to soft completion
emptying ambition through its chime
milk and bile seeping to the river source
until the insignificant unheralded
takes witless hold of everything again
and change, the servant of obscurity again and
Nothing has transcended death.

—

Hope is a flower, change is a gardener, death is the soil
Hope is irregular, death is essential, change carries all
Greed is the flower pressed, self is the garden wall
Nothing with nothing built around. Poetry is apocryphal.

The moon which over winds must travel
Hard by the warning clouds and shadows
Darling morn will come again
And fields that grow into their green

Fit with retro furniture our love
Enacts a ritual and
We are resolute—our parts
Well-written futures we rehearse

A faun undone by lust
The comedy of love
And wanting to remain intact
Despite his non-existence

London

In the Hampstead ponds
A green walk without sides

The Chiswick Garden

The cherries overripe and vile
Rotted together—wasp-eaten

Rye Harbour

A murky shelving sea recedes
Green on the pitch—lavender in grey
We could have made it here yesterday
But instead we came today.

Suddenly the SUN
A stretched Limon
Under the ice my lover
                    Comes
Under the carriage door
A soap cart foaming in the rain
All these black olives on the floor

Virtuous or not men pass away
      And souls may whisper as they go
And some are friends who say kind words
      And some deserve it so.

Her father, the doctor—happier at home
The oval window where the script is read
Give this note to Molly in the garden
For we cannot want for fantasy
In a realm where nothing in the way of real
Is to be found. A motherless daughter
In a gown of green. I do not sew. I read.

(Late of the Moscow Poems)

Her revolutionary boyfriend says:

Silence!
The crow reckons
In its comic attire
You walk like an asshole!
Old man.
I'm so tired before
I'm even born.
The Sun can't make it
This winter
We'll have to make do with this bucket
And a bottle of vodka
You say you are unhappy
Well what would happiness be
You seem to enjoy it whatever it is.
And your pants are tight
And you get fucked
The cloud wilts past
My door—and again
The light returns—opens
Like a fridge I'm in.

I have finished a moment more lasting than bronze
A fresh nothing held up to the face of Boreas
When I look for myself I am not even there
Everything has escaped through the fingers of my
    goddess
The steps built up above the peasants' slope
From which we hear the clamour of our poem
The unheard bleat of the sacrificial goat
The unheeding beauty of a stranger passing.

To his former lover:

Venus's blue muscles under her uniform
The crevice filled by the usual device
I can find no kinder way of saying it
She is without restraint or taste in matters of the flesh.

Sleep arrives with a lopsided smile
How can the tongue keep still at times like these
The legs and arms recall all former deeds
I am nowhere to be seen.

She is a brazen treasure that has buried me
I am a fool whose gold was never pure
Now with the chance to shore my stocks I see
Our meeting was the last time I had love for me.

I remember staying with Theobold who was proof that an excellent constitution is no match for a prolonged course of overfeeding. Who can love any man whose liver is out of order—and imagines himself wanting of an affectionate family?

He was a man on the verge of the greatest excitement.…the galloping hooves…

She weeps at the table in distress:

Even the Green is
Raw—the red field keels
Over if I could hide
Inside yr pain with you
Also the red wet tide
That keeps me feeling
You—no longer ever real.

A beautiful young woman is unfaithful to herself.

Essence on cardboard
non aliter—not otherwise
preserve forever that which
other wise cannot be.

Giovanni Bellini
a portrait of a boy
Venice, about 1475
oil on wood

The Bellini takes my
breath away
I see my son
and think I cannot love
this world—because
it fades irregularly
I cannot teach that
does not know even
how to love—it
is as easy as seeing
something everyone can see
the Bellini boy
faded to a fine trace
almost a veneer.

Hungry with loss
Of her the heaviest
(Empty bag—her loss)
And what to act upon
The bruise blooms purple and yellow
Like the face of a pansie
A week old flower

A pig brought in to slaughter
Zeus's daughter lost inside a dream
The summer that enwraps her shoulders
Bare now is the hour of our need.

Great limbs break off
But hang still in the trees
Held in our view. The cricket
In the kitchen for example.

The moon it doesn't even look round
Not real at all but flat and metal
Like a tin dish driven over in the street
Like a foil dish driven over in the street
I love you moon—you are everything to me.

As I was being questioned at the checkpoint I saw what I thought was Moore—running on the mountainside.

(Me and my small transgression about to be punished— and Moore, naked and alive with independence dancing beyond anybody else's claims).

Train song

We are now approaching Sunningdale
This is a Reading Train
This is Sunningdale
This Train is for Reading
The next station is Martins Heron.

The washhouse overwhelmed
By sour lips
The workhorse dragged
By ropes across the ground

What is important
(right now)
ripe vines and ants

the darkest pools
of trees, and those
were leaves

A courtesan
descending stairs
were leaves

It's my poem not yours
There's this hero—
A grass plot and
Dimensions. I'm exhausted

—

the shepherd with his goatskin
wakes empty in the sun
my mouth dried crisp—opens a future
drinks on

—

the shape of the shirt
a man who likes his lilies

—

sulphuric acid
a poet's habit
a nurse's tit
held out of reach
an inch is infinite
this is a burn right through

—

How far are the birds?
Not far. Nothing can
Leave us—nothing leaves us

And here in my wagon
We hear birds—is it a thrush
This instant—everywhere

—

once you took down the large chalice
Dawn's aurora
Like an unattended spectacle
The lilies opening
Alive but representing yesterday
My ecstasy is empty
I write this instead of anything else
Futures swing past

Some undergraduate
Wearing that scent
You wore when we met.

What was lost
the taller weeds
Rose-of-Sharon

Glow! Laud glorious—
In a fell instance—
Gravity and her smiling swound
I will come at last to rest

(still no privacy)

the teeth of blood
my mother gave to me
her apron of bleach
and arms of beef
and scent of hair
and golden yeast
to stop you cannot stop
until you rest

I sleep alone alone
I woke—this endless season
And no fit tale to mediate
(an audience might mirror my neglect)

(the truth and what she says
may casually agree
but one must understand the ways
in which they are distinct
and cannot mean the same)

If I might make a start
Once more—a misheard shaft
of light—what could compare
Art in the shape of one wrong word

Slight as the ash tree bough
Twelve of them in the chill
Glint quite still and white
Then black against the snow

A mouthful of earth
Awaits us all
Whether by fire or fall
A mouthful of dirt our final word

Your brown eyes looked
      So fond of me
But I cannot be seen
      Where I now stay
They had gold warmth
      But ringed with blue
A glow then sometimes
      Cold outside
I wanted you all through
      These years
But you weren't mine
      Nor ever were
And I could never hope
      To hold
That golden warmth
      All ringed with blue

A single glove
        dropped in the undergrowth
since I have loved you
        and you left
alone
        's not half so good

a ringed dove claps

a single glove
        left in the road

a watercolour of a fish
        its deep blue greenish fin
and watery eye, a jewel
        and red blood round the gills.
I made this for you
        thinking nothing of its life
just of the colours
        on its side
its obsolete candescent
        pride

weeping and weep no more
all takes just a moment
laughing laugh no more
this day is passing

living and no more
my heart be constant
dying and no more
to hold I cannot.

Let death her song console
With nothingness our lives
Lived in her shade. Soul
With her momentary flare
Escapes our crushing want
Our arms which are
Defenseless each to each
Reaching after that which
is its loss

The dead woman that is living here
dead in their cars, the dead
arriving home. If it were easier
to live we would all live. But to
keep an open face—only a few
(and some now dead).

—

What can I carry across to you?
My pity? Or should I take yours.
Love, which I hold onto as if it's nothing
Is nothing. I mean it is not anything

Narcissus with no mirror
The child without his mother
What should I bring to you
It will not be pity or

Our love, which I can't find
without you I must bring
my general humanity
a dull brute beast who eats

and shits, seems happy
without content or the ability
to reflect upon
loss as love's reflection.

—

Hunkered down over bleach
floors and tiles and chicken rinds
prone to bursts of varicose
and valium and anodynes

the brightest Cava Queen
whose valley echoed with the screams
of little trembling narcissi
plucked into a beaker for a Sunday offering.

—

the small house I grew up in—but still its hidden
spots—concealed in dreams and silences between
inside of me—the ceaseless
ground erupting into being

—

My mother I had thought—but no
Maybe even blood a little—stars
a cloudy night—I had high hopes
But no—not now for her—

A leaf blows heads or tails.

The long noon of the city
Honeyed Oxford and
The bones of York
Where nothing can be done

Ombersley

The Elms tower
upside down
around the black
fish pool

<u>The Battle of Britain/Cathy's Garden/</u>
<u>Oxford Ohio./2011</u>

The arbor of the garden fringe
The complex branches of the upper reaches
In between the skies
Like some brittle fossil of a living lung
The spicules fracture as
The groaning fighter crashes clumsily to earth

An old man with a lion's head
The process of his changing shape
How strange to die, how ordinary and wonderful
It was the best thing after all

Slow drips and light shower
Flat metallic sky and sombre limbs
Deer as if on set appear
And then it is again as it had been.

the rain set in
if constant motion
and emotion can be set
I have regrets
exhilarating endless rain
whether I go out or settle in
a flash of silver tears the curtain

I'm loving her in knots
I can't untangle night
As if inevitable you cannot
see yourself as separate to it
and then the afternoon
incessant bird whose song
doesn't progress—a two note threnody
So when I close my eyes
To my own thoughts I should
Have ownership in some small part
I am enslaved to that which I gave up my
    selfhood for
It is not even her—she is not anywhere
Both victims of the same hypnotic song
Two notes a threnody to morning and to afternoon.

To infinitudes
My small distempered craft
A house upon an ocean set
Or else a bird caught in a net.

Without Bastion

drunk writerless despised
as if the next inaccurate desire
of fulfilled will will offer surety
a hill fort derelict decapitates
the camp. I had ended up
leaving the ground for no
particular reason wanting only
everything. The most beautiful universe of son
eclipsed by heaviness.
Hey! come hither child, Hey!
have I just emptied all your fears
into the world. I did.

Thick May rain and thunder
on a Sunday would be August
lowering trees in lushest greens
then bright again

to end an English post-meridian

The shuttered room in sunken darks

my erection typical of the genre

blood and wine carpet to ceiling

Darling in another room. I'm gone.

Fantasia on Loss

I saw a tree felled by the bank
And thought it was a desperate fool
The saddest hunched without concern
For loss had humbled loss

Love carried her own cares
Busy between mismatched contemporaries
A child's scarf worn by a teenage girl
It is too late to meet

Child is a cavern of despair
Where light is now uncertain
Night is your companion

Take your jacket
Pen in pocket
Like a park thrown around a closet

I crawled inside your face
I cannot mean that and I do
I crawled inside of you to be there
And I could not hold the view.

—

Who are we against
The sightless faces of the dead
Our populated depths
All but the flowers and the birds
Are hindered here

Under what spectacle of light
The crowds invisible and visible
As if amongst contemporaries
Wander or resolve to stand
Between the instances of rose and wall

Light through the leaves or amber evening light
Light from the graves of others who have seen
The days of happiness and sorrow fluctuate
    like light
My day at tremble on the flat plane window
Who can or never has seen anything of this

(who in a choir of angeluses
defends himself against antiquity
who is made mad by absences
of any instant that has passed
or of his own contempt for living life

Helping himself to clumps of air
Climbing the knee deep furrows
Of indifference
Desperate though ignorant
Amidst the morbid silence of what's happening)

summermeadowshadow

Her idle attitude
Of thought her actions
I have tried to keep
Things innocent of hate
& need, and hate & need
have grown immediate
what I want I don't
know how to tell
even myself except
it is not what I get
—not even that.

All summer long

The weeks fell apart like legs
And each boy took his turn
With the indifferent summer
In a ruin of sacrifice
and sick astonishment.
At last, the last door of
The Adulthouse was opened—
At last the great whore
Of the town was naked there for them.

The muses have been
        Hear all morning
A wren, a swallow and
        A Robin
I have been confounded with
        My self-regard
And anxious over family
        And business of the world
I take no part in my success
        Or in my son's
            Near happiness
I am confounded here in
        Self-regard
            Until
A wren, some swallows and a robin
        Called.

The world scatters
Absence on my claim
To memory—a model
Of a puppet ship which
Placed upon a painted sea
As if mid journey in a
Bottle empty of its spirits
Now—all we have to show
For one long summer and
Forgetting all of it.

Every time I near myself
A death forestalls me
Knowledge such as night
Makes wisdom's vision faint
Only a planet seems
The envy of her siblings
In a sky of doubt

Struggling to keep afloat/
    As when a poem moves beyond its words
The trawler over depths/
    Into a realm impossible to read

The skiff emblazoned by the sun/
    On scattered gold and albumen
Arriving at what leaves what flowers/
    Venus the morning star, Venus the evening rose.

A modest turk
Fell off the sky
A big top tent
And trapeze act

What then is love if I am either
cognizant or else consumed?
The light like breathing
It will change.

For love has fallen
Like a misery
Upon the day—

And I remember wanting this
defenseless woods
engulfed by waves

Droitwich, late July 2011

The fruit trees are in fruit
and none should doubt
that this is summer once again
a cold cloud sky but
greens abound—the garden
pushed to the limit of its growth
and I am here again returned
to the very dwelling of my birth
and those two souls still here
and captive to their own despair
and joys—and me away now
in some absent state I hardly know.

the unused shed
takes only months to rot
with bindweed/nettle halo
overlooking poles of blistered creosote

I'm stewed under Sun—every graffitied inch
railway brick and fox piss path
(children in the psychodramas of their games)
a newt amongst detritus in a sink

Out of the corner of my eye
My mother passes
Into the undergrowth ignored
Of common evening primrose, bittercress and flax.

Fort Street, Boise, August 2011/2

My beautiful laundress
Factotum—portmanteau human
What careful task
Have you left undone

The starlings are at my door
Laughing their walks across the lawn
The lavenders in pots
Are variously dead or blossoming

<u>Suite of rain and light—London, August 2011</u>

This rain will rot your house
This is the denouement
       We've been
       Playing out

—

The light she gave me
       Her last light
That day of Endless rain
The light which
       I still see
             all silver down the
                 train window
            my son a silent
     travelling
Companion

—

In this light London
Is intoxicating
The light in London
Is intoxicating
The chivalry of war
Significant extravagance
In plumes of smoke & feathers
Rows of Terrace Houses such
       As Battersea
       & Hove

The sea deposit of a
Decorous embattled state
All parks that close at dusk
Where feral gangs of youth
Might chase an innocent to
                         death
For want of ritual.

—

This was the side of the
                 House
Which fell down—
This was the site
Where the pit grew
She fell without a word
A gasp—this wall

—

Down from the North
To sit and watch the water
When a life might any moment
out
—Burst of violens—
To kiss most lustily
The gut and bow

It is the ripped apart
Her heart which
Here in my hands—my heart
Or is it shoulder where I love
The weight, the heads held up

When I say she left her vanity behind
I just mean her mirror.

Do not suppose those things
that you feel keenly are yourself
anymore than those that leave you
speechless, dry and without incident

Death death death death
Follow it 4 times back until you understand
The lady smells of laundry whom I love
A thousand lines all hung I have pulled down—

The bride asks of the common creatures:

Who was it in passing that bestowed such beauty upon you?

Who is not devastated by this clamour?

Where is your hiding and your hunting?

Where are you as you sit invisible in the tall grass?

I have touched the squalor and the splendor of myself
And laid down tortured and in bliss
I have held myself to standards not my own
And lost all sense of common ground

A living form why grieve
As if usurped by death
Until the furthest edge leaves
One thin task left

A suite of Mirrors

Two swan that in attendance stand
Offering a sign of fortitude
Why I have chosen neither company
Nor solitude I cannot say

My head is woozie with the infinite
And so I sleep—heaped like a sideways sack
Upon a sofa that would fall if it were not
For the meager floor I rent

—

Beneath these trees love slept
Not dead but idle in her bliss
And these same trees have left
Their leaves and shadow and their breath

Oblivion plays in the foliage
One bright instant and its shade
Suns into being fall and rise
And more suns in amidst the grays

—

You loved this house you said
And I recall these walls
As if my brother's face
—but houses are immune to tenderness

without a human to inhabit them
the windows are as blind as glass
and words like love that moves the air
like motes are even more useless

—

remote oblivion dressed motherhood with love
and made the lover smile when you embrace
but memory in search of consolation after loss
could only conjure masks and not one face

catharsis pruned to self-involved avoidance
whatever she was made of she has gone
and I am left (at least) with knowing that she was
real—for now I cannot conjure anyone

—

my faith was not by faithfulness supplied
I had my love of those whose constance was
    in doubt
by also those whose love could not be tried
And both gave out

Needs must that I retreat from your opacity
For looking on you turns me too much on myself
And having want of love I gave that love to you
And giving all left nothing to receive.

—

What is this catastrophic love
That just one glance one second past
Has pushed me to the end of breath
Death is all it brings—the absolute undoing of
 a life—a precipice

But life was just display—a chance
Occurrence that might once or twice
Allow significance to coincide with incident
And so I met you and you left.

—

What care I of celebrations if the dam is gone
No time nor health secures my happiness
When all before me lacks her own one self
And I have lost all hope of (anybody) finding
 anybody else

And I again a character's unwritten part
Played out without an audience at least
The cast unproven, ill-equipped, still unrehearsed,
the curtain finally hung aloft for one short farce.

The Death of Venus

bitterness tastes green—all love
Of spring and growth that forces life
joy tastes green and so all sadnesses.
Red is the colour of our birth and death—all life
    is otherness

Trust yourself to love who love can't trust
Doubt might be the mettle of your vow
I who can not be in present time content
Can follow only rumours where she went

With each new self one learns how to be
Another lover than the one one knew
So loving leaves behind what we once were
And finding more within when new without
That which I now see clearly was unclear
That which I saw I now no longer see
As if what was a mirror darkly glazed
Now washed of all its selfish gloom reveals
A window to the world and all it holds
The light from where I sit redoubled is
And now unfogged the glass transparency
Shows more of me than I held in my haze
That which I held in vanity which was concealed
By one small mirror opens now the field.

Be not content without an outward show
If being can be anything you do—without
Contentment being is complete—but know
That in not knowing you still act your part
And can without the plot still plot your art.
So being one who knows he does not know what
Being is, you can at least read covers
though the book is never read.

<u>To Jeanne</u>

I wish you a heaven of privet scent
Of every child you ever held
Of evening light and endless dance
Of years of hours spent

Poppies

half-love half-death
as if the night held day aloft
and in the midst of green one felt a sudden burst of red
a memory grows out of death.

I'm sorry to report that all is emptiness
One might abandon hope at such a thought
Or else one might choose self-abandonment.

I prefer to carry on
in this formless eternity
And reach into the abyss
To make another cup of tea.

I'm sorry: a folly
Keats in a purple shirt, Shelley in a yellow
The afternoon upon us after play
The wine and fruit left over from tomorrow

Echo's response unheard—her lover drowning
Past the path of sunlight on the pool's frisked lid
As evening drops her frown behind the laurels
A lone cicada answered by a crow

Daughter in my arms for one more night
As lovers we shall dance outside the hall
And up against the carpark wall we might
Admit each other's need before we part

In one yard of desperation
Love wakes me
to the sea's horizon

—

I cannot stand
where I love
the ocean meets the sand

Heaven's the centre of the soul
—from *A Dialogue between Thyrsis & Dorinda*
by Andrew Marvell

To make a final composition of all time
Love in whom beauty and disaster grows
Must marry death to pass into anotherness
There ending ending and beginning grace again

On leaving my mother at Crewe Station

The bough the bird is on
A bitter winter dialect
Writ grey across the white
Somewhere in the copse is green

Somewhere underneath this scene
A summer stirs a spring
I've been thru so many winters
Will never see the like again

As with an apple for dessert
Its ordinariness sublime
I'm at a loss this day
To find another winter equal in my mind

Of all creatures best I love the birds

their soaring and their dipping flight
the whistling swallow and
~~the white-cheeked sparrow~~
~~and the colonies of feathers bright and dull,~~
~~eggs of green and speckled alabaster~~
~~nests rigged high atop~~
~~or buried underfoot~~
~~& of their rituals & courting dance, but more~~
their waking, when the day is minutes long—
their song.

to make ill of the good
what help to any man
to take a blossom down
to choke a chick in milk

it is an everyday affront

A gradual poem
(Café Rouge, Chiswick, December 23rd, 2011)

for Jeanne

There'd be nothing
That I could talk about
without

women without cancer
off the buses
women with and without

lost in the endless tumble
of exchange. Without recourse
without hope without clear memory
all tipped in the weary Thames

real material objects here at hand
and real loss of such over again
making a trip to the shop part of it
the knowledge it will go and love remain

a small hand motherly falls
a frail papered mitten that holds its pair
a tremble in spasm that cannot write
auspicious and empty with each minute shared

My mother is an antelope
What can you mean?
My mother's antelope escapes
Through which closed gate?
Her heart is free across the distant hill
And none who weep can cause her any ill.

there is nothing
like a mother
's glove—or hand
there, on my harm

taking the bus
with two of us
kicking against
the seat in front

the other children
remain other
to my small idea
of family or world.

What a damned fool it is to love
and not to love
Or else a starling holds us captive with her song
with her lament, her joy, her consternance.

Play for her tonight she cannot hear.

I noticed your mouth
Was the pit of death
An intimate space
And infinite

Your eyes one last time
To let in light
Or let out something
Silent and unseen

Your mouth that forgot
And became the grave
Like a shadow closed
And ever-growing

In the dark

In the dark-throated rattle of the night

In the mindless pain

In the tamped down hair

In the rolling eyes

In the gasps and days

She takes no consolation

Primeval loneliness

First and awful mother

Earth and night

Dusk has fallen
Right through the ground

To the women in whose
Ivy-clad realm I
Mayn't dwell

Piss of apples on the lawn
Birds of dusk—the robin
And the tit. There is nothing left

The Gardener came in and
Cleared the lot
So tired that I can not
Raise my head to see
   Who sings

Calling unseen between
   The trees

It would be Mother I
   would first call out

A church or island

Now rain is you

Did you know?

As you died

Indivisible insoluble death

Under the myrtles &

Under the myrtles &
The yews—under the
Changeless yews
and bitter asphodel
Under the privet and the haw
Nothing out of which a tree has grown

—

After the moment of release
Immediate the fall of intimate opacity
Where blood like a word spent from the mouth
Her tongue was bloody as she died

Amidst the brown fir needles
And the new heaped soil
A whisper of a breeze that might disturb the field
A word we listened for as if a word held breath

—

I have somewhere in a
Sequence of vain chemistries
Knowing the ground of love to be
An absent mother in a winterhood of light

—

This room was a railway station this bed
Replaced the bed where John Keats died

When her teeth bit down on agony
It was not the bliss of satiety alone.

The world will fall untidily to earth
For what its worth the self will settle wholly on the flesh
Night will fit exactly into day
The make-up bag she brought was buried with her body

—

An invincible sadness since first light
Wanting to leave the earth for even one instant
to enter into a realm where the self cannot follow
the flat world turned hollow

A place at last the self cannot be found
Walked into the house and found
A doorless corridor now ran
Right through the middle of the house.

—

There's a fucking monkey grin

A T.V. show

A human being

A letter unwritten and sent

A cheerio, a child in the next room
A window open for the view she cannot see

A wax doll and a crimson mouth

Dead mother with her toy

—

Up it flies to death and off it swims to death
And here the door opens to death
And in the air today the clear voice of a living death
Alone in groups of company the geese return

—

We went for lunch, for stroganoff
The day she struggled for one breath
I needed her to die
As I had booked my flight

I kept walking past people as your son
In mourning—with my head on backwards
Overgrown along the ground
Dressed in a rented suit

the green nerve-rooted trees
bits of church seen through the leaves
three men apart in black
depart across the lawn

Those who come forth
                    to cast dirt
                              Forever

Those self-elected
                    out of love
                            and theatre
Those in whose silence
                    offer
                            her last word

—

a broken-throated pigeon in a yew
a song tuned to the Malverns without view

perhaps to see the room die instantly
perhaps to see her whole family die

—

Another garden
Under drought
a stream
run out of rain

End of terrace
End of evening

—

she died inside her mouth

I fed her little bird

Breathing thru the grate

Milk all down her cheek

dredging for one breath

To mean a final thing

The desert of her mouth

The elms breathing the light

The leaves the lightest green

The blood leaving her face

The world leaving her mouth

CODA

L'una e L'altra

And now the reflection of the dark house is as real
and permanent as the house itself. The moon in the
pond or say the shadow of the Statue. Apollo in his
golden pomp.

The matter of her will no longer matters.

> *Darling* I say, stepping out into the dark
> (knowing you are not there and cannot
> hear me)— *Darling how can we go on,
> staring at some great uncanny tree?*
>   A voice which comes back to me—
> *How can we go on, how can we go on?
> What great matter are we in all this
> darkness?*
>   And the voice again—*this darkness?*
>   And that icy shard will twist—so that I
> must stay outside—alone with my pint of
> wine—and with the hope that the wind
> in the pines distracts me from the moon's
> echoes—a psychomanteum.

At her core there was either a cold rock, or a
creature terrified and hidden.

A moon blooms back at the sun—incandescent—
mordant—reclusive in the open.

A young woman trembling in her shoddy life. Her
mind a moon in retrograde.

He is terribly conscious of daily life ...his flight to the moon is in sheer desperation.

He sees the absurdity of his situation reflected in the moon's dispassionate gaze.

The moon is magnified at night ...his anxieties ... both quite stubborn, both real ...nothing to be done with either.

The way one lives, a pile of clothes and an unanswered letter, company kept with the small-minded and disillusioned. Whether light or sound, whether the moon or the Robin. Those emotions I am feeling, they are made of blood.

The moon then, her effect upon the internal and external oceans.

A lonely dream in a medieval dark.

If death was the great fear, the eternal enemy, then life was the great gift, the cherished possession... but life was nothing, historically bestowed on the ignorant and unworthy. And those making a success of this little game, they were not marked by a devotion to decency, or a signaled intelligence or bravery.

And what death promised was an end to all the ignoble and squalid concerns.

It was a matter of scale in which "I" marked the low point—and the distant clouds indicated something of the measure of the necessary escape—grand and immortal seeming, natural and ignorant. Today the clouds in dark coils seemed to hint at an inferno just beyond the horizon, a lake of flame, a lava flow, an approaching army clad in bronze and gold.